Group's®

BEST-EVER CHILDREN'S MINISTRY CLIP-ART

Group
Loveland, Colorado

Group's Best-Ever Children's Ministry Clip Art
Copyright © 1994 Group Publishing, Inc.

Credits
Edited by Jennifer Root Wilger
Cover designed by Diana Walters
Interior designed by Lisa Smith and Kari Monson
Illustrations by Amy Bryant, Jim Connolly, Victoria Twitchell Jensen, Jan Knudson, Vicki Logan, Ben Mahan, Mas Miyamoto, Lauren E. Simeone, Bron Smith, Nancy Tobin, Corbin Hillam, Charles Hogarth, Kari Monson, and Jean Bruns

Library of Congress Cataloging-in-Publication Data
Group's best-ever children's ministry clip art / [edited by Jennifer
 Root Wilger].
     p.   cm.
   ISBN 1-55945-273-0
   1. Church work with children. 2. Clip art. I. Wilger, Jennifer
Root. II. Group Publishing. III. Title: Best-ever children's ministry
clip art.
BV639.C4G76 1994
259'.22–dc20   94-13931
                                                              CIP

11 10 9 8 7 6 5 4   04 03 02 01 00 99

Printed in the United States of America.
Visit our Web site: www.grouppublishing.com

CONTENTS

INTRODUCTION

Wigglers, gigglers, talkers, listeners. Smilers, criers, runners, walkers. Your ministry is full of children of all shapes and sizes, and you have to design publications that will reach them all!

Group's Best-Ever Children's Ministry Clip Art will give a professional look to *all* the programs in your children's ministry—from cradle roll to cherub choir to after-school ice-cream socials. The children in your ministry will love having their own special artwork, and you'll love the sparkle clip art adds to your publications. Use clip art for newsletters, fliers, name tags, greeting cards, calendars, invitations—you can even photocopy the clip art onto adhesive-backed paper and create your own stickers.

Just follow the steps below to create publications that will make your people sit up and take notice.

1. Collect the information you want to include. Keep it short and to the point. Don't forget to list "the big three": **time, date, and place.**

2. Select art for the item or event you want to illustrate. The index on page 173 lists specific topics illustrated in this book. The art is divided into the following categories:

  ✳ All God's Creatures
  ✳ Preschool Play
  ✳ Special Days
  ✳ Going to Church
  ✳ Kids' World
  ✳ Bible Friends

3. Type the information (or generate it on your computer) in the form you want, leaving room for the artwork. Think about creative ways to place the art above, below, or around the text. Check your typewritten work carefully for clarity and accuracy.

4. Clip the right size of art. If you have a photocopier with enlargement and reduction capabilities, use it to create the exact size of art you need.

5. Glue the art into place. Using rubber cement will allow you to adjust the art without tearing it.

6. Duplicate and distribute the information. Watch and pray for great results!

ALL GOD'S CREATURES

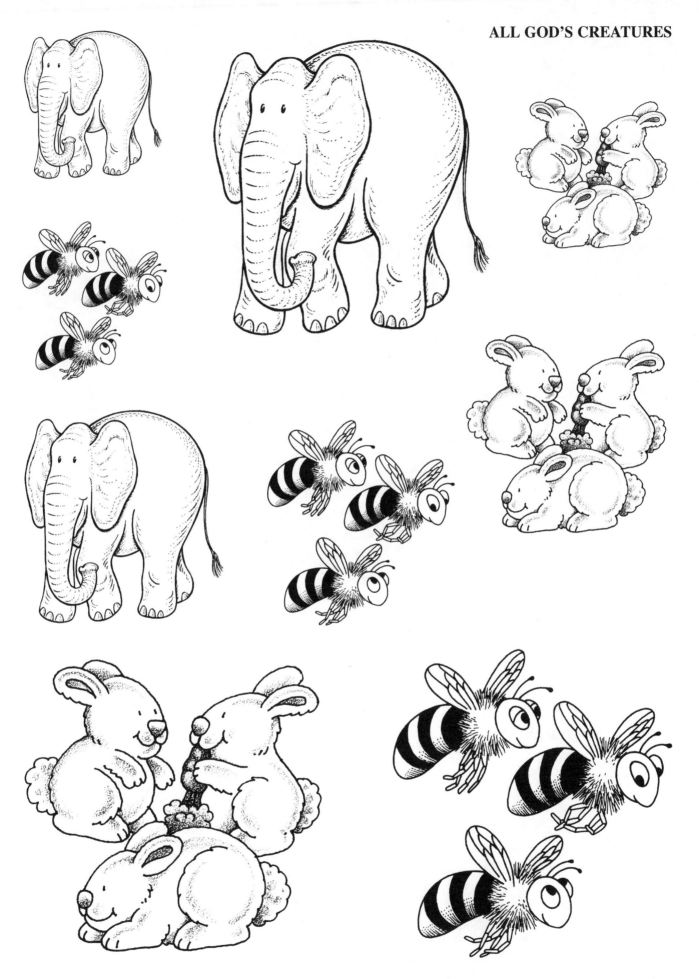

PRESCHOOL PLAY

CRADLE ROLL

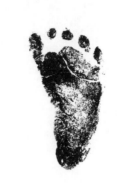

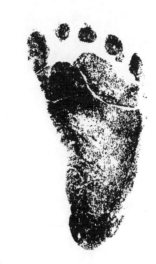

CRADLE ROLL

SPECIAL DAYS

0 1 2 3 4
5 6 7 8 9

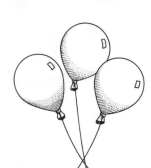

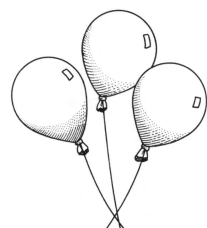

❄JANUARY

❄JANUARY

❄JANUARY

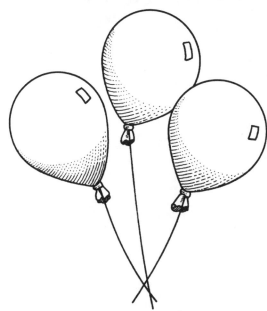

February

February

February

Good Friday

Love †one †another

Love †one †another

Good Friday

Good Friday

Love †one †another

EASTER
PAGEANT

HOSANNA!

EASTER
PAGEANT

EASTER
PAGEANT

HOSANNA!

HOSANNA!

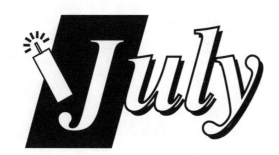

BACK TO SCHOOL

BACK TO SCHOOL

AUGUST

AUGUST

AUGUST

BACK TO SCHOOL

AUGUST

SEPTEMBER

SEPTEMBER

SEPTEMBER

ADVENT

ADVENT

ADVENT

CHRISTMAS PAGEANT

DECEMBER

DECEMBER

CHRISTMAS PAGEANT

CHRISTMAS PAGEANT

DECEMBER

welcome Lord Jesus

welcome Lord Jesus

welcome Lord Jesus

GOING TO CHURCH

God is Love

God is Love

 Bible School

 Bible School

God is Love

 Bible School

thanks!

MOM's Night Out

thanks!

MOM's Night Out

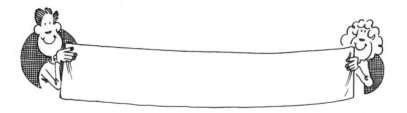

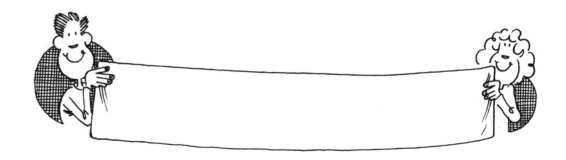

MOM's Night Out

thanks!

VOLUNTEERS

VOLUNTEERS NEEDED

HELP Wanted

VOLUNTEERS

VOLUNTEERS

VOLUNTEERS NEEDED

VOLUNTEERS NEEDED

Christening

Baptism

Baptism

Baptism

Christening

Christening

Welcome
to the Family

Dedication

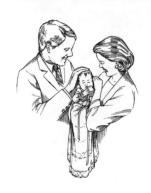

Dedication

Welcome
to the Family

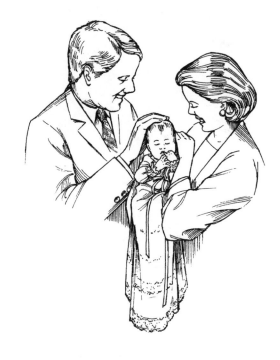

Dedication

Welcome
to the Family

 Church School

 Church School

CHILDREN'S CHURCH

CHILDREN'S CHURCH

 Church School

CHILDREN'S CHURCH

Bible Club

Bible Club

Bible Club

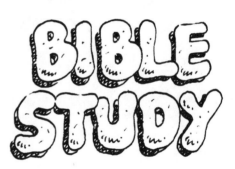

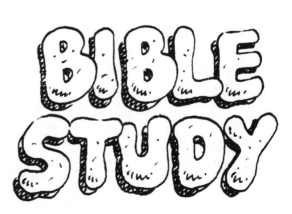

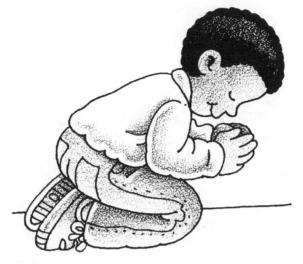

CHILDREN'S CHURCH

CHILDREN'S CHURCH

CHILDREN'S CHURCH

JESUS CARES

JESUS CARES

Bring your Friends

Bring your Friends

JESUS CARES

Bring your Friends

RALLY DAY

Come Unto Me

Church LEAGUE

Church LEAGUE

Come Unto Me

RALLY DAY

Come Unto Me

Church LEAGUE

RALLY DAY

KIDS' WORLD

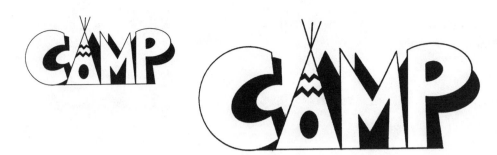

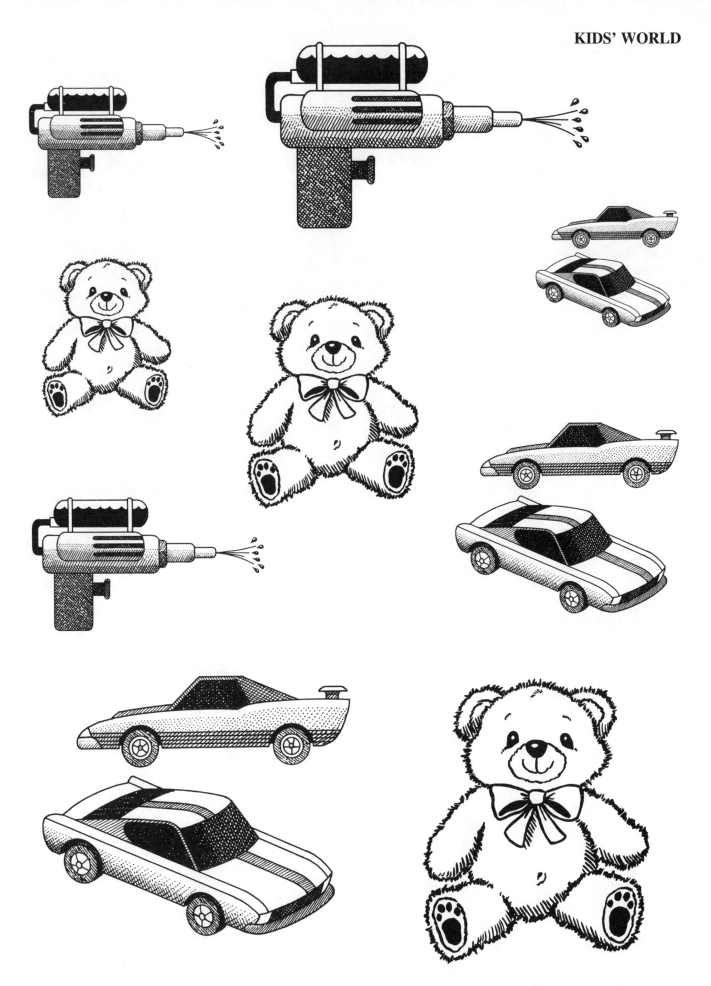

KIDS' CLUB

KIDS' CLUB

ELEMENTARY SCHOOL

ELEMENTARY SCHOOL

ELEMENTARY
SCHOOL

Awesome

AWESOME

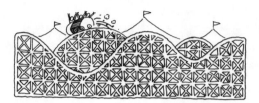

Cool

Cool

AWESOME

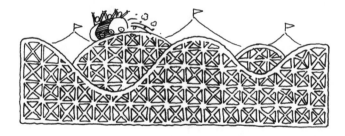

Cool

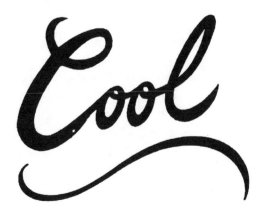

Make a joyful Noise!

Make a joyful Noise!

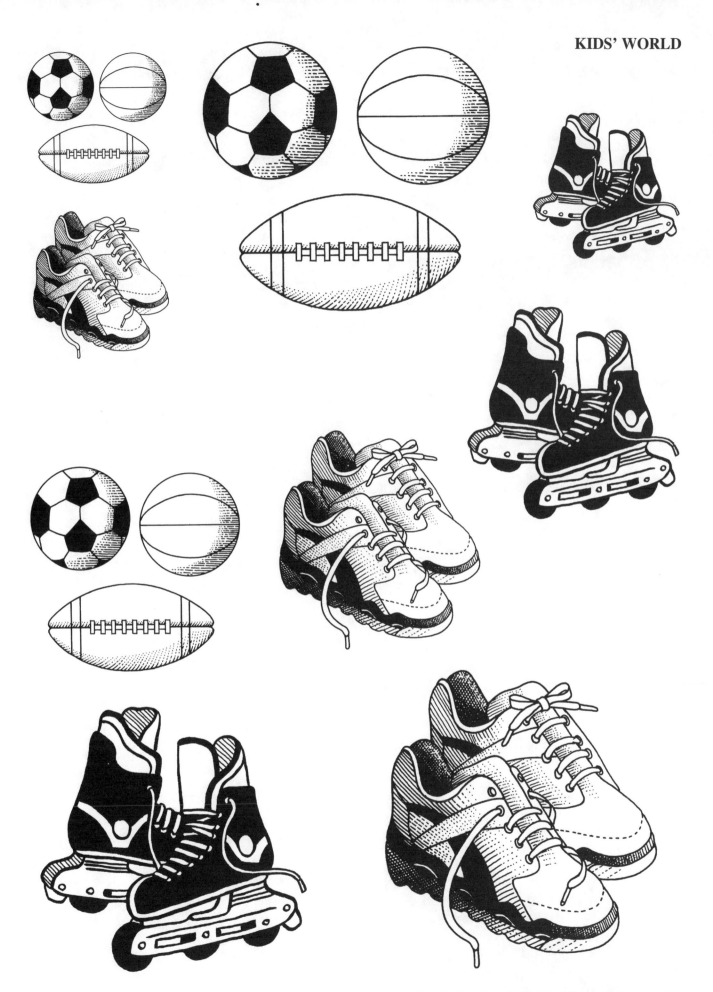

LOOK
WHAT'S
HAPPENIN'

LOOK
WHAT'S
HAPPENIN'

LOOK
WHAT'S
HAPPENIN'

Day Camp

Day Camp

Day Camp

BIBLE FRIENDS

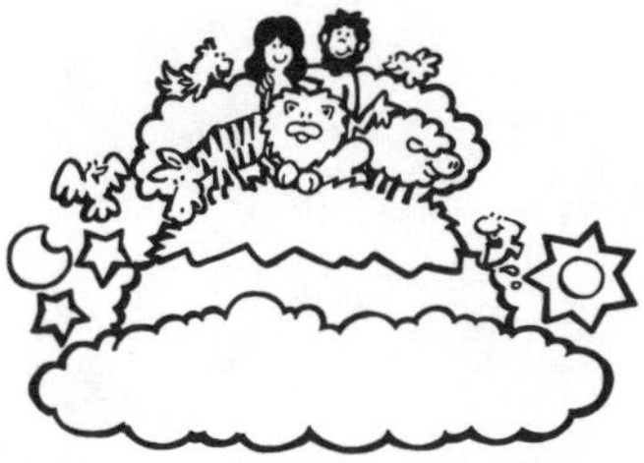

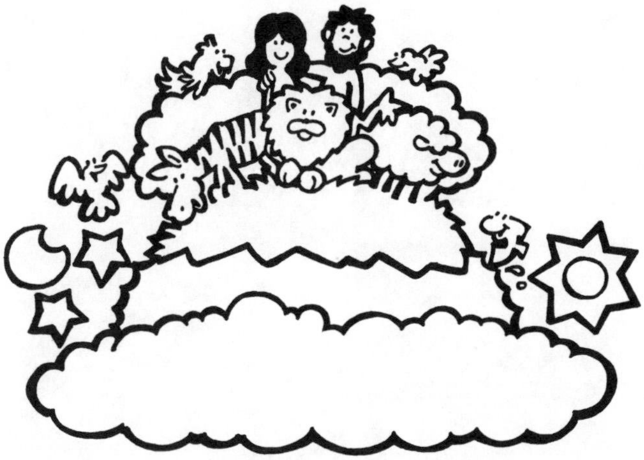

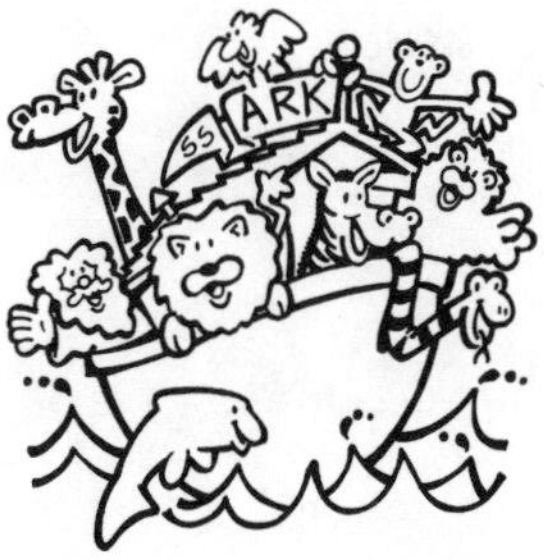

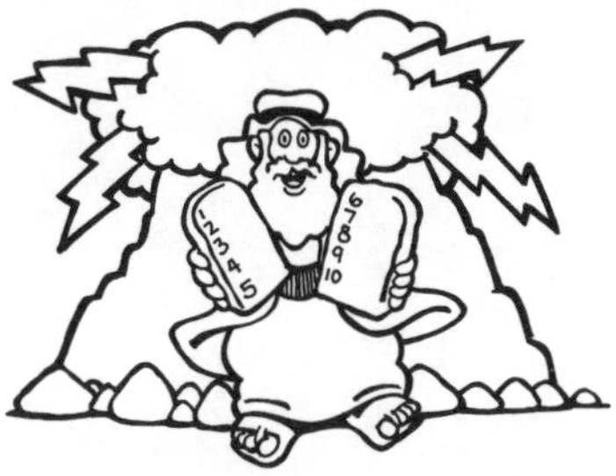

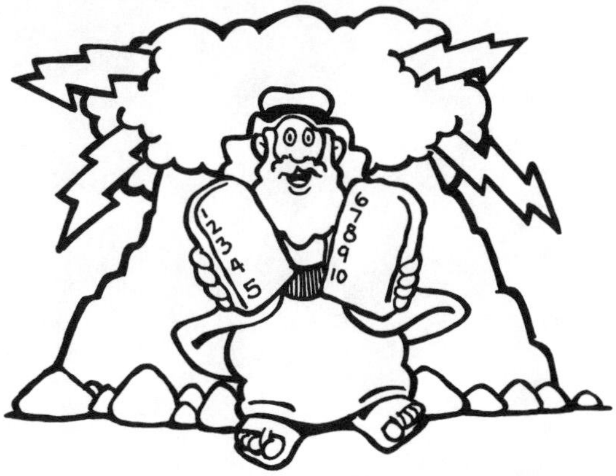

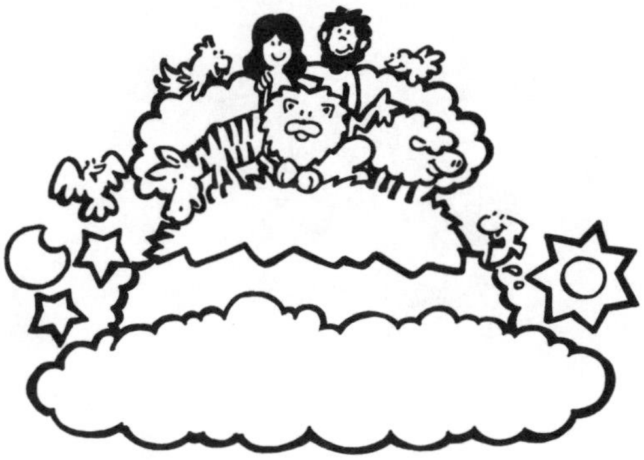

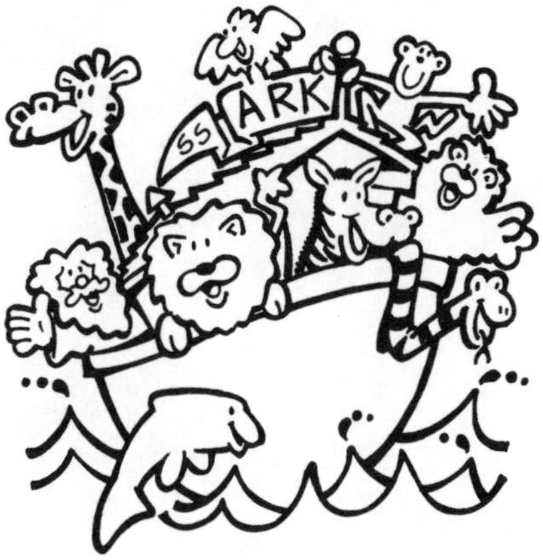
ARK

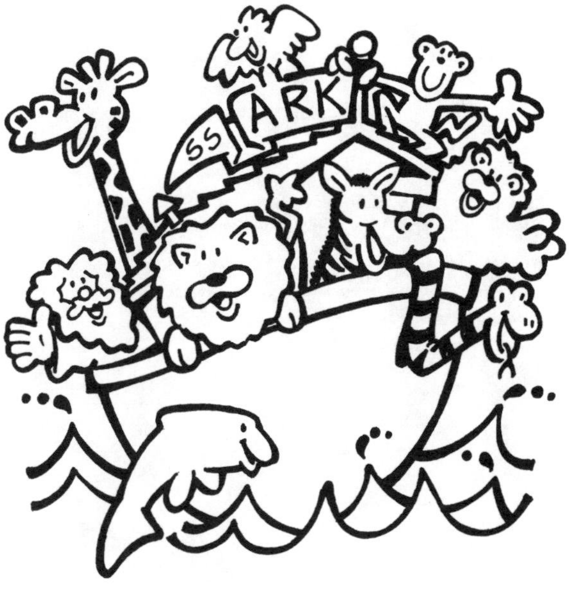
ARK
SS

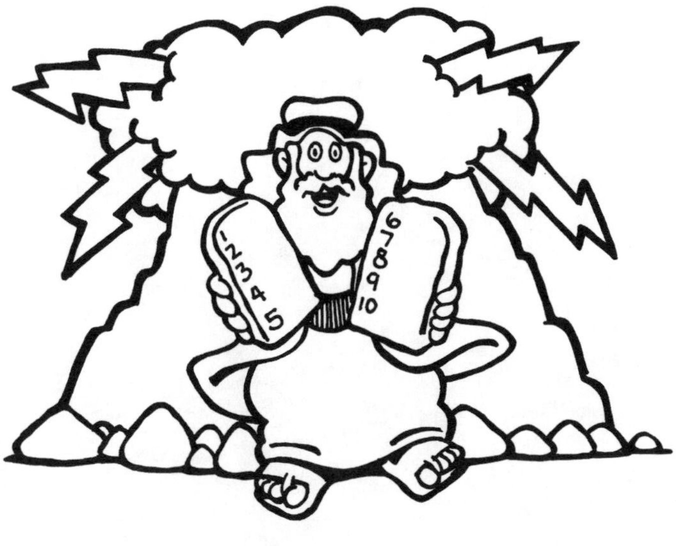
12345
678910

InDex

A

Advent, 77
Angels, 79
April, 51
August, 65
Awesome, 129

B

Baby, 23
Baby bottle, 25
Baby food, 23
Baby Jesus, 81, 163
Baby sleeping, 31, 37
Baby toys, 31, 33
Back to school, 65
Ball, 31, 133
Balloons, 45
Baptism, 99
Baseball, 149
Basketball, 133
Beach, 65
Bees, 9
Best friends, 139, 143
Bible, 89, 107
Bible club, 107
Bible school, 89
Bible study, 109
Bicycles, 155
Birthday, 43
Birthday cake, 43
Blank banner, 91
Blanket, 23
Blocks, 29
Book, 39

Bring your friends, 113
Bus, 147
Butterflies, 15

C

Camp, 119
Caterpillar, 13
Chalkboard, 151
Chicks, 13
Children's church, 105, 111, 113
Christening, 99
Christmas, 77, 79, 81, 83, 85
Christmas caroling, 83
Christmas pageant, 81
Christmas tree, 83
Christmas tree ornament, 83
Church camp, 147
Church league, 115
Church school, 105
Church social, 97
Circus, 145
Clock, 45
Come unto me, 115
Cool, 129
Cornucopia, 71
Cradle roll, 37
Crawling, 29, 35
Creation, 169
Crib, 31
Cross, 53

D

Daniel, 161
David and Goliath, 171
Day camp, 147
December, 81
Dedication, 99, 101
Diaper bag, 23
Doll, 27
Ducks, 11

E

Easter, 53, 55, 57
Easter basket, 57
Easter pageant, 57
Elementary school, 127
Elephant, 9
Empty tomb, 167

F

Fall, 67, 69, 71, 73, 75
Fall festival, 69
Father, 19, 61, 107, 119
Father's Day, 61
February, 47
Feeding the 5,000, 165
Fiery furnace, 161
Fish, 15
Fishing, 119
Football, 133
Footprint, 37